SHIFT
SHIFT

Leading Change with
Human-Centered Innovation

Kristine Merz

SHIFT: Leading Change with Human-Centered Innovation

Prominence Publishing
www.prominencepublishing.com

The author can be reached as follows:
kristine@orangesquare.com

Book editing by: Doug Brown

Book design and illustrations by: Juli Leonard

SHIFT: Leading Change with Human-Centered Innovation / Kristine Merz
1st ed.

ISBN: 978-1-988925-45-5

Dedication

This book is dedicated to every leader who has never done things the way everyone else has, and to all those who have helped me on this journey of discovery and growth.

It is also dedicated to every person with dyslexia who has an amazing mind that processes information differently and brings critical value to business with the strength of dyslexic thinking.

This book would not have been possible without the dedication and support of Doug Brown, my editor, and Juli Leonard, my designer. I have deep gratitude for their outstanding talents and gifts, which allowed me to convey these important concepts. I am thankful for all of my colleagues who gave me critical feedback. And to my wife, Patty, whose insight, wisdom, patience, and support sustain me every day.

Contents

Introduction

It's official: the Fourth Industrial Revolution has arrived. We're fusing the physical, digital and biological, designing the world around us in ways never before possible. This most radical transition will pervade all aspects of life, including of course business. We can no longer simply choose a way forward, we must design a way forward based on a human-centered approach to innovation. In other words, we must not be reactive but reflective. We will need to develop new skills and habits, taking the time to listen carefully to customers, employees and outside partners — to really truly listen — before bolting into action. We will need to learn new ways of applying the principles and practices of design thinking to ensure the value we create is human-centered. We will need to learn how to embrace failure, frustration and change as steps on the path to true innovation. Most fundamentally, we must shift from corporate-centered thinking to human-centered thinking and invert our focus from problem-solving to problem-finding.

Over the course of my career as I have moved from

graphic designer to creative director, entrepreneur, business owner, business strategist, and leader, I have had the pleasure of working for many different for-profit and nonprofit clients. Each presents distinct needs and challenges. And yet so many times I was handed a problem whose solution was not going to achieve the intended outcome. Albert Einstein once famously said: "If I were given one hour to save the planet, I would spend 59 minutes defining the problem and one minute resolving it." But in business — where time is money and action feels like progress — we tend to cut to the chase, often only to discover too far down the road that we're chasing after the wrong thing.

We have all experienced this, investing time and energy in solving the wrong problem and therefore failing to achieve our actual goal — and ironically losing time and money in the process. In business (and in life), people often make the mistake of assuming that the goal is money. But when we move from a corporate-centered approach to a human-centered approach, profit becomes not so much the goal as the consequence of purpose-driven work that meets customers' needs.

We stand now at a moment of tremendous change. Businesses that adapt will succeed and those that do not will fail. But change is scary and more often than not our response to it is reactive. But if instead we can reel in the fear and take the time to reflect carefully, we can design our way toward a business model that puts people first.

Designing for Change: Shifting from a Corporate-Centered Approach to a Human-Centered Approach

Increasingly we're hearing about the Fourth Industrial Revolution and the monumental changes already occurring in every sector of life. For many of us in the business world, negotiating those changes can feel like a life — or death — proposition. The prospect of such an overwhelming threat tends to provoke rash responses borne out of a sense of urgency. But for businesses to evolve successfully, the process has to be deeply reflective, a dwelling in the very uncomfortable place of the unknown. This requires a commitment to making time to listen, understand, learn, explore, and emphasize.

This process can't be hurried or executed by force of will. Businesses have to fight the urge to move quickly from problem to solution.

Businesses will have to have the skills to search themselves and evolve in a way that's organic and therefore authentic. A quick fix imposed from within will only ring false. Instead, businesses will have to work from within to ask themselves essential questions.

"Who are we now?"

"What do we want to do now?"

"What do our customers actually want and need now?"

"Do we have to rethink our mission?"

To answer such questions effectively, businesses will have to engage in a difficult process, one that requires serious insight and vision and takes bold leadership. This book aims to engage you in that process.

"There's a myth that time is money. In fact, time is more precious than money. It's a nonrenewable resource. Once you've spent it, and if you've spent it badly, it's gone forever."

—Neil A. Fiore

Changes

As a formally trained graphic designer with my own creative services firm, I thought my role would be to apply the most fundamental principle I learned in design school.

"You can't find a solution until you have a clear idea of what the problem is."

It turns out I was wrong. No one was interested in spending time finding problems — clients thought they knew what the problem was when they hired us. Our job was not to ask probing questions to find the right problem but to design solutions.

Back in 1992, when I entered the business world, human-centered design thinking was not on anyone's radar.

Businesses were operating on a corporate-centered, dominance-driven model focused solely on revenue growth and profitability.

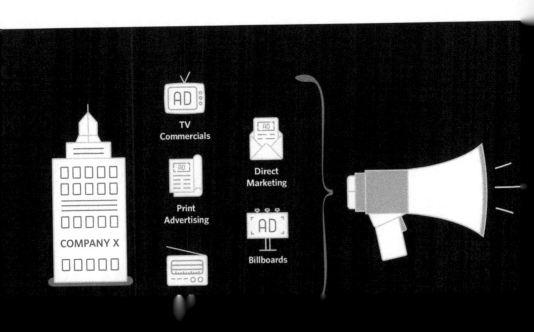

They were using one-way marketing communication channels (such as TV and radio commercials, print advertising, direct marketing, billboards).

Over the last quarter-century, much has changed, most notably how digital technology has forced two-way communications between businesses and clients. The resulting collection of data has, in turn, forced businesses to adopt a more human-centered approach.

The next shift in the evolution toward an increasingly human-centered approach is the social enterprise business model, where companies have to care about more than just revenue, growth, and profitability. This model focuses on social responsibility, the natural environment, and the stakeholder network. Indeed, businesses today are increasingly putting people first and listening to people both inside and outside the organization and promoting a high degree of collaboration and transparency at every level.

So, my story — that is, the experience I'm drawing from — is fundamentally about change, both in form and content. I've weathered economic changes and paradigm shifts in my own area of business, and from a *graphic* design to a *business* design firm.

New market conditions of course sometimes require change. One may have no choice but to adapt or perish. But even as I did that, I kept at the center of my practice the understanding that if you don't take the time to *identify the right problem to solve*, you'll get the wrong answer, and in the process waste a lot of time and money.

Ultimately what I recognize as most crucially true is that businesses that fail to shift from a corporate-centered to a human-centered approach are most likely to spend the most time addressing the wrong problems.

By corporate-centered, what I mean is a practice wherein businesses think primarily from their point of view, arriving at decisions, practices and services that they then try to foist on customers rather than beginning with asking how they can best meet their customers' needs.

I believe we must turn the current culture of problem-solving on its head and shift to a culture of problem-finding, wherein businesses dedicate sufficient time to that process, identifying the many problems that need to be solved to achieve a desired goal.

It is in this exploratory process that you stand to discover invisible problems you otherwise wouldn't have seen, problems that may well have eventually surfaced at a time when their solutions would be harder to enact.

My experience has shown me two things:

1 Old habits die hard — and while the death of patriarchal corporate-centered thinking is underway, it's far from writhing in its final throes. (Here's to soon saying goodbye to the end of what I like to call "The Age of BS".)

2 Understanding design or human-centered thinking is one thing, but embracing the practice, another altogether. It requires change — and difficult change at that.

Brand Is More Than Just Visual Identity

Branding today is no longer simply how we distinguish one company from another. For a brand to resonate, it has to engage with its customers: it's defined by what *they* think, not merely what *you* think.

As a designer, I was in charge of designing the look and feel of a brand, the visual identity that distinguishes one company from others. In other words, I was responsible for creating the *visual expression* of that company. In the early stages, I worked on the logo — the ultimate visual distillation that serves as the instant recall mechanism of any brand. Then I designed the other brand identity elements: the colors, fonts, icons, image style, and so on. Next, I moved on to designing the entire brand identity system, applying it to the collection of marketing elements that work together to create all of the unified, consistent and flexible brand assets. Finally, I developed the brand standards — the guidelines and rules that describe and define how to create and protect a firm's brand identity.

You learn a lot about a business when you're tasked with the creation of visual expression. The fundamental thing I learned was that visual design was considered a late-stage consideration, a process of pretty-making. Even when clients saw it as relatively necessary, it was never as important to them as finance or business strategy around growth and profitability.

But brand identity isn't merely a "look" a designer creates; it's predicated on a coherent philosophy, and core beliefs that pervade all business practices.

If a designer is tasked with capturing the concept of transparency, then the business better, in fact, *be* transparent. Identity is a company's visual expression of who it truly is; it is fundamental/inner inside truth projected to the outside world.

At junctures of significant change, taking the time to gain new clarity on the core truth a business is focused on allows for a more powerful brand identity and positioning in the market. Such a process can't be half-hearted. If any of the BS, top-down, corporate-centered ways of thinking from the past are brought forward, they'll be starkly evident.

The unspoken comedy of the character of Jack Donaghy on *30 Rock* was that he was a dinosaur and he didn't know it. He was still carrying on as though he could call the shots and the world would bend to his will.

Today, customers call the shots — and they'll call you out plenty fast if your brand doesn't ring true.

What has worked in the past is not going to work for the future. For example, you cannot rely on internal knowledge and the experience of your leadership team to identify the problems to solve. For companies to stay relevant, you need a new cultural radar that is outwardly directed and allows you to learn and listen to keep pace with the changes and disruptions that will impact your business.

Part of the challenge for many leaders is to recognize qualities that make you the dinosaur in the room. You can't know what you don't know, as the saying goes, but you can find new tools and methods to understand what that might be. To do that requires being vulnerable enough to listen, to try new things and fail trying, learn, try again until you succeed. If you are not failing, you are playing it to safe.

Change is hard. My journey now is to make a difference by bringing clarity to changing brands and to lead the conversation on designing a new way forward. Integral to that will be defining brand strategy and the concept of brand as more than just visual identity and giving the significance of that understanding as much attention as revenue targets and other financial goals.

THE JOURNEY TO A VISUAL IDENTITY

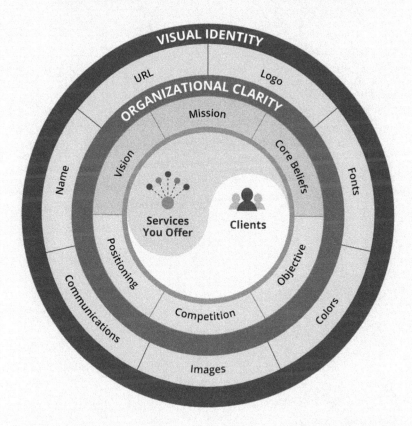

Visual Identity starts with the core — the fit between the services you offer and the value they bring to clients — value propositions. This is framed by the six elements of organizational clarity. Three are internal: vision, mission and core beliefs. Three are external: positioning, competition, and objectives. This leads to the look and feel of your brand — the way your organization presents itself — is your visual identity.

It should project four things:

1. Who you are.
2. What you do.
3. How you do it.
4. Where you want to go.

When the Boom Went Bust

Before I started my company, Orange Square, in 2002, I'd been working for a firm in a small town outside of Boston. The office was chic with modern exposed brick, designer furniture, an open floor plan — what you would expect from a design firm. The firm had a staff of around 30 people and was growing fast. It was well known for its brand identity work in the New England/Boston market and created award-winning brands along with accompanying marketing communication. At the height of the dot-com bubble, opportunities seemed boundless and the office thrummed with energy.

Then the boom went bust. We lost clients and had to lower our fees, and it was clear that the good times had come to an end. Flush, the firm had grown top heavy, and so for me the writing was on the wall: it was time to cut bait.

But my time there was instructive. I learned a lot about money during the dot-com boom. Fees didn't always correlate with the dimensions of the job being done. Pricing had more to do with relationships than with value. True, there was at times something magical about the terms of negotiation: with the right pitch, outrageous fees could be charged. These were not necessarily positive lessons. The murkiness of the ethics was clear to me then as it is now.

Nevertheless, I created more brands in those two years than I ever thought possible, and in that process, I learned that doing corporate-centered work can extinguish your humanity. When I was working with start-ups building a company/brand when the focus was to sell or make as much money as fast as they could, I felt duplicitous, as though I was just building a brand facade, a glittering attraction designed not to serve people but to put one over on them by convincing them some new digital approach had actual value. Focused solely on potential sales, the brands I was working on had no soul.

To my way of thinking, for work to feel meaningful and for business-to-business services to have value for people, you need to do more than just set financial goals. You have to make people your principal concern. I understand that for a for-profit company, shareholders are important stakeholders, but making them more important than your customers comes at the expense of research and development, at the expense of any long-term vision based on values and market understanding — and ultimately disappointing the very same shareholders. It's how you end up with so many broken systems.

Over time I have learned about the profound differences in the impact of corporate-centered and human-centered approaches when building brands. The brands I was working on in the dot-com boom were corporate-centered. The companies were looking at a "market opportunity," and they had to move fast to be the first to market to capture it. Market opportunities were suddenly outlandishly huge, and the allure of all that money was for many intoxicating.

LET ME GIVE YOU AN EXAMPLE

One of the brands I developed was a Customer Relationship Management software company

(please remember this was in 2000 and such business technology solutions didn't exist).
The market opportunity was as big as companies chose to envision *and* portray it.

Here was an instance of near-universal need. Every business in just about every sector needed to manage its customers better. With this new digital Customer Relationship Management software, you could manage customers in nuanced ways, *and* on a scale no one had ever previously imagined. The pitch for this software couldn't have been more obvious: If your competition uses this software and manages its customers better than you... well, it's belly up for you.

So here was a product with obvious need and value, *and* a killer sales pitch. What could go wrong? Well, add audacity and greed to the mix. By setting an astronomical financial sales goal at the outset, all efforts were geared toward meeting that goal rather than serving clients and thereby their customers. Big-time investors flocked to the opportunity, and the company, bloated on capital, had to find a way to deliver a return when instead it should have been focused on the particular needs of the client's customers.

Coming from a corporate-centered approach, these companies would "prove" the "need" by defining the market opportunity as if *everyone* could or would buy the software they were developing. Then that big number would become the financial target, essentially defining what was possible setting the bar unrealistically high. This is how and why during the dot-com boom, so many companies got tons of money and investors. But was it possible to meet the projected numbers? This corporate-centered market opportunity approach meant that employees had to work day and night to try to reach a financial goal and capitalize on the theoretically huge market opportunity.

And then there's the other problem with this approach: building the product. They were developing the Customer Relationship Management software for a market opportunity or "market needs," but not for any one particular customer or their customers' needs. In this corporate-centered paradigm, they focused on an industry in the most general of terms to the exclusion of specifics that define and differentiate one business from the next. By building it for everyone, they were in effect, building it for no one.

Collision with Reality — When Corporate-Centered Thinking Meets Its Customer Base

A human-centered or design thinking approach, on the other hand, starts with a focus on understanding the needs of a specific business and its customers. The company I described above was being driven by projections of astronomic sales — i.e., wealth — so they designed a system that would theoretically meet *everyone's* needs. This, in turn, made the software more expensive to develop and more complex to navigate. Such systems invariably prove cumbersome, and often the function that was supposed to be streamlined for the customer ends up creating a whole new kind of a headache. Add to that the fundamental fact that the transition to digital technology was in itself already a radical departure from the old way of doing business, and you can imagine the resistance such complexity engendered. In the midst of that frustration, customers couldn't help but reflect on the promises that had been made, the dream they'd been sold, and the very real money they'd spent on it.

This is why, when you come from a place of corporate-centered thinking, it is so hard to build an authentic brand that resonates with a company — its employees and its customers.

Yes, you can develop the mission, vision, and values for such companies — I did. You can name the company/brand, make a logo and create an entire visual identity system and all of the marketing materials — I did that too. You can hire all of the people you need to build the product, sell the product and run the company — they did. But did they, in the end, achieve their financial goal? No, not even close. Were they successful? This depends on how you define success. They sold software and had customers, but in time they, like most of the companies in the dot-com boom that took a corporate-centered approach, went bust. This was not because they weren't first to market. It was not because they had not developed a potentially useful product. It was because their approach was all wrong. They focused on profit instead of people.

We humans have a knack for story. It's integral to our species. The people taking this corporate-centered approach were in effect telling themselves *and* others a story. As fantastical as it may seem now, at the time they may well have believed their projections, and so they were able to make fabulous promises to investors, employees, and clients alike.

This internal corporate thinking, this drinking the Kool-Aid, isn't necessarily duplicitous. Rather, it's delusional. These were businesses I no longer wanted to build brands for or help market. By launching my own company, I could make different choices about the kinds of customers we would have. I wanted to tell a story — but one that was true. And meaningful.

For me, it was rather as though I'd stumbled onto a stage set where everything looks entirely plausible — there's an *office,* and it's really nice looking, and there are lots of professional people busy at work, and there's a feeling in the air, a sense of exciting belief in the mission. And now without even knowing it, I've been conscripted to share in this story, to create a logo and a visual identity for them that conveys not just the function of their product but the ethos of the company. I have now unwittingly become one of the cascading effects. And moreover, by giving material form to their story and designing a visual identity, I've made matters worse by making their flawed vision a seeming reality. Everybody is now even more energized. The thing they've been working so hard to make real now seems real. In our little closed feedback loop, everything is just wonderful.

When this closed feedback loop of internal corporate thinking intersects with what customers will actually buy, and it becomes clear that the sales goals will not be met — that is, when the company finally collides with reality — it's forced to rethink the viability of the funding strategy and the financial goals it projected. It's ultimately this crisis moment that begins to force human-centered thinking.

If it is at this point that you start to understand customer needs in relation to your product or services, it's too late.

You took the wrong approach and are now faced with making corrections, establishing new goals, trying different approaches, adjusting the company's message and marketing internally and externally. Because Joe Smith and his leadership team developed a company and sold a product based not on the specific needs of clients but on their own avarice, things didn't go as planned.

Every step of the way, corporate-centered thinking drove the company farther away from anything that would offer valuable solutions to customer problems — which, in the end, is what truly matters.

SHIFT

It's Worth Pausing for a Moment to Review the Cascading Effects of Corporate-Centered Thinking:

1. In this instance, the company started with an idea for a customer-relationship software product that would work for anyone who needed to manage customers. This — theoretically — presented a large market opportunity.

2. Based on that large market opportunity, they set an audacious financial goal and cultivated investors based on that goal.

3. They built their company on this thinking, on a story that came to seem palpably real, a story that informed critical decisions. They hired employees and built a company around the story based on their financial goal.

4. Designers designed a brand identity that reflected that goal.

5. Employees worked day and night trying to achieve that goal.

6. Marketing materials told the story of that goal.

7. Programmers and designers built the software product for that "fantastic" market opportunity, that supposedly universal "need."

8. The sales strategy and marketing materials were thus designed to target that projected opportunity.

9. The brand then collided with customer reality and things came to a screeching halt.

10. As a result, lots of time and money had to be spent on:
    - Understanding that reality: Why were things not going as planned?
    - Trying to understand why they couldn't meet their goals.

- Communicating that reality and disappointing investors.
- Employees living that depressing reality — and sometimes getting blamed for it.
- Re-conceiving goals — trying to find ones they thought they could meet but still not knowing what they were.
- Developing new marketing messaging and strategy.
- Changing all of the marketing materials.
- Selling based on these new messages.
- Learning what worked and what did not in the new strategy and goals.
- Investing more money.
- Struggling more.

Truth in Branding

People are emotional, intuitive beings, and that's the level on which I speak to them in my branding.

A brand is a gut feeling.

It has to ring true. It can't merely enlist others in telling a lie or a fable. Now, the lie or fable may well not be intentional — it could be something the company *wants* to be true — but that matters little to customers. Or, eventually, to employees, who will soon recognize the falsity of the vision, mission, and values. No amount of training or persuasion will change what employees know and feel.

In time, the company went out of business. Investors lost money. Employees who had toiled long hours did not get the money and success they'd been promised. In the case I described, after having dedicated long hard hours to the cause, employees had to negotiate tremendous deflation then somehow and find a way to soldier on. But soldiering on is not the same as working with genuine dedication on something you truly believe in. And when leadership reveals it does not truly espouse or live the values it claims to, no amount of internal marketing communications can hide that fact. That too is a costly consequence of corporate-centered thinking: the loss of staff morale. In the end, brands are made by individual employees, not companies or markets. And they need to believe in the mission throughout the process. For that to happen, the mission must be grounded in the reality of what customers need.

FOR A COMPANY TO SUCCEED IN BRANDING, TO PRODUCE A GUT FEELING THAT RINGS TRUE:

1. Its product or service has to continually bring real value to customers, which in turn engenders customer loyalty.

2. That loyalty is enhanced by the performance of individual employees who work with customers initially and in follow-up meetings.

In other words, meaningful relationships are formed. On a higher level yet, a company might earn distinctions for its work and thought leadership. This leads to trust — the very foundation of a brand.

Corporate-centered thinking creates a disconnect between the company's inside truth and the needs of the outside world. This type of thinking forgets that both customers and employees are what matter most.

Understanding individual human needs must always be where you start and end. It should not be something where, late in the game, you realize your products and services are challenging to sell or that the value you thought they had are different from what your customers need.

SHIFT

Find the Right Problem

Businesses will always be looking for an opportunity or market need. The difference between opportunity and need is that an opportunity will expire or change, while a true basic human need does not. But even when you are using human-centered thinking and working to meet a human need, you still need to make sure you are using a *problem-finding approach*.

LET'S TAKE THE HUMAN NEED TO SIT.

- What problem is the person trying to solve aside from sitting?

- How do they want to sit?

- Why do they want to sit?

- Do they want to sit?

- For how long do they want to sit?

- What do they need to do while they are sitting?

There's a multitude of human factors that can inform the types of chairs the market may need. The market opportunity for people who need to sit is huge. But forming business goals based on so amorphous an opportunity is not only risky but the most expensive and difficult road to travel.

Corporate-centered thinking is the old way of thinking, but I still see people in companies setting goals using this approach. I don't think smart leaders have bad intentions; I think they may simply be entrenched in that way of thinking without adequately understanding its cascading effects.

Smart leaders can and need to become bold leaders. Part of being a courageous leader is the willingness to slow things down to find the right problems to solve that will generate authentic growth.

As I've mentioned, we are seeing a real paradigm shift: Products can no longer be foisted on people. Customer feedback now drives everything. But in the business-to-business world, sales can be more complex, with multiple decision-makers, so it is not as easy to conceive of a single customer, and therefore a single customer's needs.

For example, a contract research organization selling clinical trial services to a pharma company is selling high-value, complex services with multiple decision-makers in different parts of the pharma company.

Who they're selling to isn't singular, and thus the feedback loop is kaleidoscopic rather than linear: there's no easy data set to review to get clear answers about what customers need and don't need. In such a case, taking a human-centered approach can be hard, and it's easy to understand the temptation to lapse into old ways of doing business, of deciding what the problem is so you can solve it.

It's not until you can clearly see the true cost of corporate-centered thinking on both the bottom line profits and employees' morale that you'll be willing to commit to the rigor and grit a human-centered model requires — and that way find the right problems, and solve them.

I have spent a large part of my career (at times without even knowing it) arriving at an understanding of the difference between corporate-centered thinking and human-centered thinking.

I want to share how to design a new
way forward for business by first
defining clearly a human-centered
problem and setting goals based on
that, and then, rather than jumping
to problem solving, focusing on
problem finding by interrogating
assumptions, inviting different points
of view, allowing for the possibility
that you may be fundamentally
mistaken. Though difficult, this is a
far better approach in the long run
than the quick rush-to-the-buck of
corporate-centered thinking.

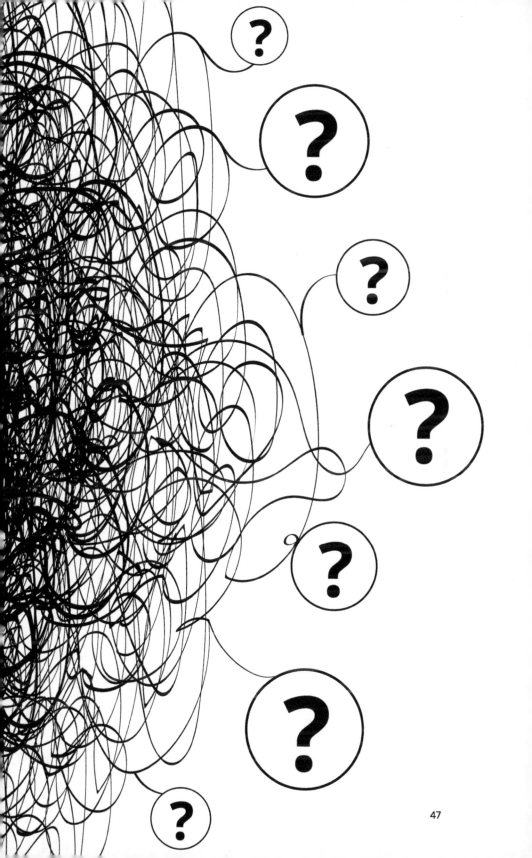

When the Solution Is the Problem

There are three types of problems:

SIMPLE PROBLEMS

You Know
the Problem

You Know
the Solution

COMPLEX PROBLEMS

You Know
the Problem

You Don't Know
the Solution

INVISIBLE PROBLEMS

You Don't Know
the Problem

You Don't Know
the Solution

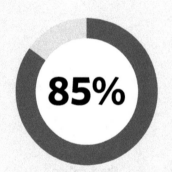

85%

85% of C-suite executives admit they are bad at problem diagnosis.[1]

1 Wedell-Wedellsborg, Thomas. "Are You Solving the Right Problems?" Harvard Business Review, 18 Jan. 2017, hbr.org/2017/01/are-you-solving-the-right-problems.

Which comes as no great surprise, since there's not much of a culture of problem finding in the business world. But that oversight is significant indeed.

My experience has taught me that the invisible or hidden problems are the ones that sink a project and drive significant costs. They're under the surface. To uncover them, you have to do the work.

All three problem types — simple, complex and invisible — are in play at all times.

Most people focus on complex problems, where they have identified the problem, but they don't know the solution. Instead, as you work on solutions to complex problems, your focus should be to look for the invisible problems. You should also continually ask yourself whether you're solving the right problem in the first place.

With AI decoding customer feedback and accelerating the understanding of customer behavior, the customer really is king. The shift here is radical, in terms not just of business practices but of professional identity. For a CEO to face the possibility that his — or less probably her — authority is no longer the core basis of decision-making is rather like kings of yore coming to terms with their loss of divinely sanctioned rule.

The simple fact is that we live in a world of proliferating information. It is no longer possible for a person or a company to control the narrative (about its content or its volume); it's now a free-for-all Internet/social media conversation. For the conversation to be productive for companies, they have to listen — and that includes CEOs.

When I began my career in design, I thought I could use my training as a designer to solve complex corporate problems. More than a quarter-century of experience has taught me that corporate dynamics are such that new ideas aren't always welcome.

I want to help train today's business leaders to shift away from corporate-centered thinking and achieve the growth and innovation they seek by setting goals from a human-centered perspective. I want to teach you how to design a new way forward and achieve greater success with less counter-productive struggle.

In other words, I want to make sure you don't set about trying to solve the wrong problem and waste precious time and resources in getting the wrong answer.

If 85% of C-suite executives surveyed agreed that their companies are bad at problem diagnosis and even more, 87% said this carried significant costs, it would seem fairly obvious that they don't have a culture of problem finding, just a culture of problem-solving.

106 C-suite executives surveyed[2]
(representing 91 private and public-sector companies in 17 countries)

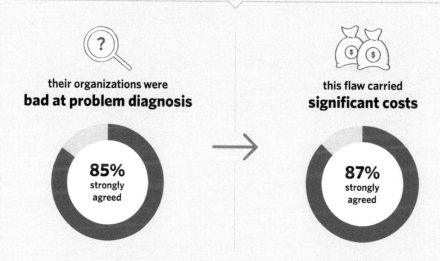

their organizations were
bad at problem diagnosis

this flaw carried
significant costs

85%
strongly
agreed

→

87%
strongly
agreed

IT SEEMS FAIRLY OBVIOUS THAT THERE ISN'T A CULTURE OF PROBLEM FINDING, JUST A CULTURE OF PROBLEM-SOLVING.

2 Wedell-Wedellsborg, Thomas. "Are You Solving the Right Problems?" Harvard Business Review, 18 Jan. 2017, hbr.org/2017/01/are-you-solving-the-right-problems.

Whether your goal is to transform, create something new or grow, the bottom line is this: if you set about solving the wrong problem, you will get the wrong solution. Which is why, when you're trying to achieve a goal, the first thing you must do is listen — truly listen — so you can understand and focus on your current clients' pain points. Problem-solving can't properly begin until there's true clarity on what is the right problem to solve.

No One Said It Would Be Easy

As theoretically apparent as this may seem, its actual practice by actual human beings can be quite difficult. People are eager to move from problem to solution because it's gratifying. We want to move away from all of the negative feelings we have when faced with a problem.

Problems are hard. They make you sit in the very uncomfortable place of "not knowing." This requires what the Romantic poet John Keats called "negative capability," the ability to be "in uncertainties."[3] Problems also bring up the possibility of failure. But the biggest challenge is that solving problems correctly requires you to be vulnerable. The faster we can move away from the feelings that come up when we are not satisfied and move toward solving them, the better. But the faster we move on, the more likely we are to be moving on in the wrong direction.

3 Fessler, Leah. "A 19th-century poet's trick for cultivating a creative mindset" Quartz, 22 Mar. 2017, https://qz.com/938847/john-keats-theory-of-negative-capability-can-help-you-cultivate-a-creative-mindset.

Some feelings when your needs are not satisfied

Angry	**Embarrassed**	**Tense**
Enraged	Ashamed	Nervous
Furious	Flustered	Anxious
Irate	Mortified	Cranky
Livid	Self-Conscious	Distressed
Outraged	Guilty	Edgy
Resentful	Chagrined	Stressed Out

Confused	**Annoyed**	**Fatigue**
Ambivalent	Aggravated	Beat
Baffled	Frustrated	Burnt Out
Lost	Impatient	Exhausted
Perplexed	Irritated	Tired
Puzzled	Irked	Warn Out
Torn	Dismayed	Depleted

Vulnerable	**Afraid**	**Sad**
Helpless	Panicked	Dejected
Insecure	Apprehensive	Despair
Reserved	Dread	Disappointed
Shaky	Scared	Hopeless
Guarded	Worried	Unhappy
Fragile	Petrified	Depressed

Aversion	**Pain**	**Disquiet**
Contempt	Agony	Alarmed
Disgusted	Grief	Disturbed
Dislike	Hurt	Surprised
Hate	Lonely	Upset
Horrified	Miserable	Restless
Hostile	Devastated	Rattled

Remember

When you solve the wrong problem, you get the wrong solution, which in turn costs you and every employee in your company time and money.

Instead, you must dwell with rigor and grit in uncertainty — "love the questions," as the German-language poet Rainer Maria Rilke said. We have to sit with the feelings that come up when we are not satisfied. We must not grasp after quick solutions but work to understand the true nature of our problem. This is what I call problem finding. To do this takes guts and decisiveness, and real leadership that's responsive *and* responsible. And to fail to do indicates nothing so much as a lack of precisely that.

Introduce failure as an acceptable by-product of not-knowing.

Corporate culture and corporate structure, however, are set up to solve problems, not find them. They reward bold, decisive action — and then put it in a PowerPoint slide. While in some sense this is a form of "failing fast," it's not quite the same as doing so mindfully — that is, embracing failure as a way to learn.

NEED PROOF? TAKE THIS QUIZ

1. Can you name five ways you celebrate and reward failure in your company?

2. Are there opportunities for employees to share their stories of what they learned by failing?

3. How do you reward employees for spending time finding problems rather than solving them?

4. Do you provide training on the importance of failure in your work?

5. Can you cite two key stories your company tells where C-suite executives modeled vulnerability and failure on the path to success?

6. Do you give employees time not to have the answer?

7. Do you leave time for a pause, that is, the time where you set the problem aside, and avail yourself of the chance for an idea simply to come to you unbidden?

NOTES:

Find the Hidden Problems

1. **Once you have stated a goal, consider it from another perspective** to challenge assumptions.

    Example: If you're a man, describe it from a woman's viewpoint and vice versa. How can you change the way you are looking at your idea?

2. **Restate the problem and break it into parts**, then rearrange the components and develop a new version.

    Example: You have to organize a big presentation with many different speakers. Break up the presentation's sections and rearrange them in front of you to see whether there's actually a different way to tell the story. Reassign the different parts to the different speakers and imagine their take on the subject.

3. **Collaborate across silos.** Different points of view will offer new perspectives and new definitions of the problem you are solving.

Example: Don't be afraid to ask people at all levels of the organization their opinion, as new ideas can be generated from anywhere. At an award-winning, world-class magazine (COLORS), editorial meetings included EVERYONE including the receptionist and sometimes the water delivery guy if they bribed him with coffee. They got some of their best ideas this way.

4. **Go outside your sector** and look for something similar but in a different industry to find ideas and a new point of view.

   Example: Elon Musk wants to build a colony on Mars because he knows that will inspire ideas nobody would think of if focused only on technology needed on Earth. If you work in the business-to-business world, look at what consumer goods companies are doing and vice versa.

5. **Sit in the unknown.** That's where ideas come from. That's where you'll find what you don't know.

   Example: Did an idea ever pop into your head in the shower? This is a time when a lot of people experience epiphanies because they're not really 'in gear' yet, and when they're not actively thinking about the problem, a new idea comes to them because they've cleared their mind of noise and clutter.

6. Allow yourself and everyone on the team to **be vulnerable**. Embrace, as Brene Brown says, "the willingness to be 'all in' even when you know it can mean failing." Create failing events where you compete in two teams who comes up with the most 'failed' ideas. If it helps, consider Thomas Edison's famous line: *"I haven't **failed** — I've just found 10,000 ways that won't work."*

7. Make your ideas visible. Have everyone sketch or draw what they think you are working on and compare for differences and similarities. You'll gain a new understanding of what you are trying to solve and discover you don't all have the same vision. Words are subject to a wide range of interpretations; images make meaning visible.

8. Define the problem, then restate it from different customers' points of view. Be sure to give the customers real names and make them as 'real' as

possible so you can connect with them. If you want to have some fun, do some live prototyping and have a workshop where people act out the customer scenarios.

9. **Deliberately thinking about something can often be counter-productive.** Tell someone to say something funny or something insightful and watch how they freeze. Sometimes we just need to go do something else. Even just taking a five-minute walk and coming back can make a difference. In that time, watch for thoughts that pop into your head and write them down.

10. **Start from the desired endpoint and work your way back to the problem.** Try to come up with at least three other problems the endpoint could solve.

11. **Be curious.** Ask lots of different questions. Act like a three-year-old, ask a question, answer it then say why over and over.

12. **Write ideas on index cards or sticky notes and make a wall of ideas that you can leave up and live**

with over time. What patterns do you see? What do others not working on the project see? Invite people to put a dot on each of the ones they think are most intriguing/important so you can start to see what is standing out to others.

13. **When you think you have the answers, find some one with a totally different point of view** and invite them into the process. Do not get defensive or try to defend your point of view. Entertain all opinions.

14. **Listen without interrupting.** When a person is being cut off with defensive remarks, they shrink. When a person instead feels they are being truly heard, they shine and produce their best ideas.

Ultimately, all of this work is in service of answering the most fundamental — and vital — question: **Are you solving the right problem or have you found a more important one you need to address?**

Building Models Focusing on Vulnerability as a Core Strength

After years of hard work, reflection, and research, I am utterly convinced that vulnerability is the wellspring of creativity, innovation, and change, and achieving your goals in the Fourth Industrial Revolution will not only require a human-centered approach but a change in culture. In *What Makes a Great Leader?* [4] Daniel Goleman shows us that emotional intelligence has been found to be twice as important as technical skills and IQ. That means a company must build a culture of celebrating and embracing vulnerability, starting with the C-suite.

Companies that build models around vulnerability will be more successful at designing a new path forward using design-based thinking and co-creation — the act of creating with stakeholders to ensure you understand their needs. As digital, physical, and our own biological systems merge and radically change

4 Goleman, Daniel. "Emotional Intelligence" Daniel Goleman, http://www.danielgoleman.info/topics/emotional-intelligence.

These functions of business are all in flux.

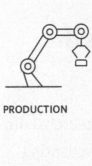
PRODUCTION

MANAGEMENT

GOVERNANCE

TRAINING

HIRING

OPERATIONS

PURCHASING

SALES CONVERSION

LEAD GENERATION

SAFETY

So the question is:
How are you going to not merely deal with this monumental change but understand it and engage with it productively?

what it means to be human, all facets of business are evolving.

Fundamental to this is appreciating that a position of authority in no way correlates with a monopoly on knowledge. Once you begin to lead with a full appreciation of that, all kinds of creative options become possible, because you're not intent on having all the answers, on being the boss or the smartest person in the room. Instead you're seeking to lead by modeling vulnerability, inspiring curiosity and risk-taking among your staff, and knowing not only that people will fail, but that failure is a crucial part of the work. Work in a way that embodies and fosters that ethos.

Linear thinking, corporate-centered thinking, top-down management — these are all concepts born of an industrial age, an age of rigid power structures.

Today, we see in the family, in education and in the workplace ever greater fluidity. Respect has grown more mutual — earned through kindness, intelligence, creativity — and roles more fluid. That very same

CORPORATE-CENTERED THINKING ————————————————

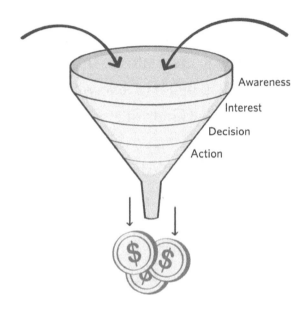

LINEAR THINKING ————————————————

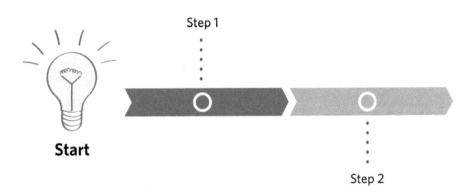

TOP-DOWN MANAGEMENT

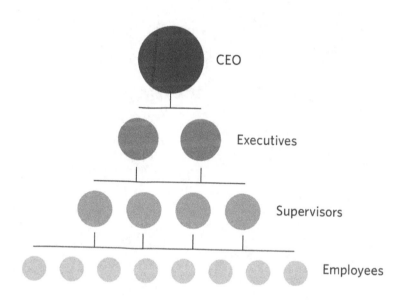

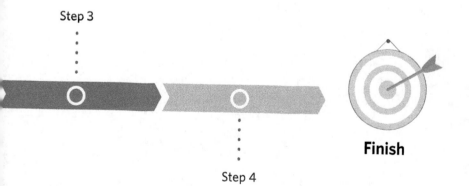

If a CEO can say frankly and simply "I don't know" and "we might fail, and that's OK," a world of possibilities opens for those who may in fact know, or at least have the beginnings of an idea. They're liberated. And it all starts with the modeling of vulnerability at the top.

dynamic of social interplay is, as we have seen, likewise at play in business, as customers increasingly drive business decisions. Making all of that possible is the proliferation of available information and influential communication platforms.

And yet, far too many companies are still, by their own CEO's admission, poor at problem diagnosis. But what are they doing about that? The issue is not merely a matter of logistics; it's a matter of conceptualization, of dwelling in the vulnerability of not knowing long enough to begin to move in the right direction. This requires the one thing each of us feels we have less of every day: time.

I believe you can no longer simply choose a way forward, you must design a way forward based on a human-centered approach to innovation. You have to listen to customers, employees, outside partners — **really listen** — before bolting into action. In applying the principles and practices of design to ensure you create new value and new forms of competitive advantage, you must build a culture of vulnerability. To do that as a leader, you must learn how to embrace failure, problems, and change as they are the steps on the way to true innovation.

An Eye Toward the Future

Designers are addicted to change. Let's face it: without change we wouldn't have a job. Because change is where problems come from, and designers are chronic problem solvers, I cannot tell you how excited I am to be living in the Fourth Industrial Revolution.

The speed, scale, and force of this change are like nothing we have ever before seen. We're all experiencing it in different ways:

- Moving from two-dimensional to three-dimensional printing.

- From understanding biology to hacking biology with gene editing and reprogramming DNA.

- From traditional manufacturing to nanotechnology in advanced manufacturing such as putting nanoparticles in fabric to kill bacteria, making clothes odor-resistant.

- From traditional drug delivery to nanoparticles to deliver drugs, heat, light or other substances to specific types of cells, such as cancer cells.

- From human learning to machine learning to artificial intelligence.

At times the acceleration of the Fourth Industrial Revolution — its pace and our lack of control over it — will feel overwhelming.

Looking back at all three industrial revolutions, it's hard to say precisely when one ends and the next begins, but overall the clear trend is that of acceleration. At each stage, humans have used advanced technology to solve problems, and the duration of each revolution has grown shorter.

Each industrial revolution has been about making the impossible possible. In the Fourth Industrial Revolution, we are fusing the physical, digital and biological worlds, giving us the ability to design the world around us in ways that were never before possible. It is this complex integrated ability that will only further accelerate change. This will also cause a sharp increase in invisible problems, things we just don't know because we have never experienced anything like what this current/new future holds.

We will continue to see disruptions in entire industries and business models. Every day, more manual processes become automated, and as technology continues to accelerate, so will automation and advancement in automation, all of which will disrupt the labor market on a monumental scale. It already is.

On a more individual scale, changes in customer expectations and the rapid development of products (products that once took a year to develop will see "hackathons" put the equivalent to market a week later) will drive business principles and practices. But ultimately, it's people — business leaders and politicians/policymakers — who will decide the shape these changes take. I'd go so far as to say that it's dangerous to imagine that technology *causes* change; people cause change. We make decisions for better or worse. We can always choose the direction our future moves in.

The Four Industrial Revolutions

1760 - 1885

1885 - 1970

125 Years
Industry 1.0

- Mechanization
- Steam Power
- Weaving Loom

85 Years
Industry 2.0

- Mass Production
- Assembly Line
- Electricity

It's hard to say precisely when one industrial revolution ends and the next begins.

1970 - 2015

2015 - Present

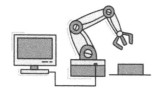

45 Years
Industry 3.0

- Automation
- Computing
- Electronics

Ongoing
Industry 4.0

- Cyber-Physical Systems
- Internet of Things
- Networks
- Artificial Intelligence

Customers are increasingly at the epicenter of the economy, and "delighting them" will get harder and harder, particularly in the business-to-business setting. The problems being solved are not easy, and the systems that need to change — health care for example — are so complex and broken that scrapping everything is not possible. Sometimes "delighting the customer" seems all but impossible.

This is where radical disruption comes in. In some parts of the world, we're seeing it now in banking, with the emergence of neo-banks designing innovative user experiences. In France, the standard process for opening a bank account requires you to go to the bank, have a meeting and then wait for days. The bank Nickle allows you to open an account in a few minutes.

In the UK, Tide is focused on giving business owners their time back and you can get approved for a loan of up to £150,000 in under two minutes, with no early repayment fees or impact on credit scores. And what was/is the fundamental problem with traditional banking? It views customers as an exploitable resource. What in effect do the new banks seek to do? Delight their customers. Perhaps as well as any example — indeed may be certainly better than any example — the banking industry exemplifies practices that stem from a business assuming that they provide a service everyone needs and so can dictate the terms of that service. Until someone comes along and does it better, and thereby changes expectations. Zappos did it with not just free returns but what feels like a truly personal customer-service focus. Thanks to Amazon, we expect things to be delivered "overnight," and now in some parts of the country within an hour.

Today, in the Fourth Industrial Revolution, we're creating a new story about how we want to live, and these changes will affect the very essence of what it means to be human. So there's a lot at stake.

As exciting as that may seem, the reality is that people don't like change. In fact, most hate it. As business leaders, we have to ensure that as we move forward, we don't leave others behind.

People REALLY hate change for at least three reasons.

1. Change always brings up the clear possibility of failure, as well as the possibility that you won't be able to control the change that ensues.

2. No one likes to sit in the uncomfort-able place of "not knowing," which making change requires.

3. Change requires you to be vulnerable, as your uncertainty is communicated to others and can be seen as a weakness.

My Own Story of Change

I have had my brand consultancy and design firm for
17 years, but I have been in creative services business
— as a designer, then art director, creative director,
and strategist — for almost three decades. In that
time, I have seen and experienced lots of change in
business. In fact, at my firm, we have become experts
at helping businesses navigate significant points
of change with regard to their brand. As a consultant,
I have the benefit of having an outside perspective,
while in my own business, I do not. Nevertheless,
I could see that if I continued in the same direction,
things weren't likely to end well.

SEEING THE END OF THE ROAD

One day I came across an AdAge article[5] that painted
a picture of a change that had happened in my industry
and that I was unaware of. In 2014, the list of the ten
largest advertising agencies in the world shifted. For
the first time, not one but *four* consulting firms showed

5 Schultz, E.J. "The Race is On!" Ad Age, http://adage.com/article/news/consultancies-rising/308845.

up on this list: Accenture, PwC, IBM, and Deloitte.
This was shocking: when you think of companies like
these, you don't think of them as advertising agencies.
Yet these large companies had expanded their services,
and it only took a small piece of their total business
— data analytics applied to advertising — to create
a massive disruption. All sectors experience disruptive
change at some point, but this was a tectonic shift of
which I had been entirely unaware. It was astounding.
These firms were not advertising agencies, but they
had profoundly disrupted the advertising industry in
short order.

Around that same time, Blair Enns wrote a provocative
post[6], "Is the design firm an endangered species?"
In this post, he talks about the three types of business
designers are actually in: marketing, internal communications, and product development. His overall point
was that design firms need to choose to be only one
of these types of businesses, and that design is just a
component rather than a product in itself. I knew
when I read this it was true because so many firms like
mine started the same way I did as a designer. He was
making a clear distinction between the business you
are in and the application of design in that business.

6 Blair, Enns. "Is The Design Firm an Endangered Species?" Win Without Pitching, https://www.winwithout-pitching.com/design-firms.

At the time, my firm offered two out of three —
marketing and internal communications. The bulk
of our work was developing strategies, designing
brand identities, and executing all of the many
brand touchpoints, all of the various marketing
communication campaigns, and print and digital
materials. Blair defined internal communications
as helping clients communicate internally with
employees and people affiliated with the company.
We did this as well and in many forms.

IN EFFECT, BLAIR WAS SAYING TWO THINGS:

1. If you are holding onto the idea of selling "design-
   thinking" or "design" as a general concept,
   stability will elude you. I had recognized this years
   ago, which was why we were working in those
   two types of businesses.

2. You have to choose just one type of business.

WHICH GOT ME TO THINKING.

The future of marketing and selling was turning into
more of a data analytics game. I could build more
services in response to that, but that would never get
me out of bed in the morning. I had avoided the

commodity side of marketing for years, so why would I do it now? As for the second facet of the business, internal communications, I had no interest in doing that 100% of the time, so my answer was no to either one.

NOW WHAT?

I was at a crossroads. I had a few choices: close shop and find something new to do with my skills, keep going as I was and let the business run its course, or face the change I needed to make to my business. In effect, I had to do for myself what I do for others, negotiating change by asking the right questions about who I am and what I want, what the market is and what it wants, and how I can best integrate those two concerns.

I see this disruptive change as yet another example of the shift from "the old guard" to "the new guard." In this case, the "old guard" are the advertising agencies that continued to do business the standard way, creating compelling advertising and marketing messages for different advertising channels. The "old guard" thinking was that brands were built by advertising and marketing. It's only human nature to think what you do makes a difference and drives a market. But the new reality is that customers, not brands, drive business.

The primary drivers of the disruption in advertising were the Internet, new technology, and new delivery channels. Many of the old one-way advertising channels (TV commercials, billboards) are still around, but the Internet and technology brought new channels and two-way communication platforms. The new guard recognizes that brands are built through an amalgamation of customer experiences — experiences that we can now track, which produces lots and lots of data. Companies like Accenture, PwC, IBM, and Deloitte had the advantage of looking at advertising and marketing from a different perspective, and one in which they already had significant expertise.

When you think of disruption and the concept of "the old guard" vs. "the new guard," it's important to note that change comes in many forms. Some disruption comes from new, innovative business models like Airbnb or Lyft. Others come from well-established businesses finding relevance in new markets. It helps not to think of the new *guard* as new *companies*:

change can come from the established ones as well —
as Accenture and IBM demonstrate. You have to stay
curious, always on the lookout, always open to new
ideas and new technologies. It's how you stand to find
that vital piece of information or make that critical
connection that keeps you from being overtaken by
change and instead empowered by an understanding
of the nature of the change before you.

**So I chose to face the change head-on. Here are
the first two questions that came to mind when I
assessed how to respond to that disruption of my
industry:**

1. What does this mean for my company?

2. What changes do we need to make?

As a designer, I have been practicing "design thinking"
for 27 years. As I've said, one of the core principles
of my training is that you can't find the right solution
until you have a clear understanding of what the
true problem is. This may sound simple, but so often
companies identify the wrong problem — and get the
wrong answer.

If I had simply identified the problem in our industry
as the use of business data analytics, then my solution
might have been to find a way to add data analytics
services to my firm's portfolio of services.

Such a reaction would have been representative of
one of the critical mistakes businesses make today.
They see the change and disruption in terms of what
the other companies that scooped them offer and
then set about adding those services to their business.
This often leads to wasted time and money.

In my case, if I had added data analytic services,
I would have needed to build a modern marketing
communications firm, which would have involved
a tremendous investment of time and money. But
was that really the solution? Was that really the right
problem to solve? And how would I ever compete
with established behemoths that had vastly more
experience, capital and firepower?

In business when you're suddenly made aware of the
change you didn't see coming, particularly one that
feels disruptive, there's a reflexive lurch to close the

gap between yourself and the new dynamic — it's a kind of panic, like a sucker punch in the stomach, really.

In that moment it's easy to lose sight of who you are, what makes you unique, what you want, and what has made you successful thus far. You may imagine that you have a clear understanding of the problem you are facing, but the change you see is not always the problem you should be focused on. Remember, you can't find the right solution until you have a clear idea of what the problem *really* is.

So, addressing my situation from a problem-finding approach rather than a problem-solving one, I asked myself two questions:

1. What do I want to do?

2. Is what I have done in the past what I want to continue to do in the future?

When we act according to what we think we *should* do, we risk disavowing what it is that we, in fact, *want* to do. It's as though we imagine we have no choice in the matter, in effect relinquishing responsibility. This conception of business as driven purely by market forces and not actual human beings is yet another expression of corporate thinking. Human-centered thinking accounts for desire. Desire allows you to own your choices and feel empowered by that.

In that sequence of questions, you can see how a process of refinement takes place. A question doesn't simply yield an answer, it begets another question.

Those are very different from the first two questions that had come to mind, which I stated earlier:

Q1: What does this mean for our company (that data analytics has taken over marketing)?

Q2: What changes do we need to make? (A: Add data analytics to our company.)

When I asked myself the questions using a problem-finding approach, things became clear.

Q: Do we want to do data analytics?

A: No. I did not start a creative services firm to focus on data.

In this part of the process, I let the "no's" help me find a yes.

Challenge Your Perspective

Disruption is an opportunity to change your company's perspective on the challenge it faces. When you change your perspective, you can innovate and develop new ideas. Instead of letting disruption induce panic, let disruption open your mind to all kinds of new possibilities. Ask questions based on a problem-finding approach rather than a problem-solving approach. The goal is not to race to the quickest "solution" to quell the anxiety of change, but to explore freely without the pressure of quickly getting "the right answer."

Get into a startup spirit, that curious open-minded-ness that might even feel naive and yet enables the free flow of ideas, the generative sense that there are no dumb questions or wrong answers, without fear of failure. Stick with it, don't judge or on the other hand feel too satisfied too soon, just keep generating lots of ideas from the questions you pose.

Unlike a startup, you can draw from experience, from the knowledge and wisdom you've gained over time. Inside your company, you have expert employees with different points of view. Collaborate across different silos to hear those different points of view and thereby better identify and diagnose problems you may not even be aware of. And while you are doing that, don't forget what your company is truly great at now — indeed let that be the wellspring of new ideas.

In addition to yourself and your employees, the last and most important groups you can use in the problem-finding process are your clients, suppliers, and consultants. Those relationships are vital. As a consultant to large companies myself, I think we are the most underutilized resource when it comes to this type of thinking. My firm has completed over 290 projects for one company and we have worked with every business unit in it. We have a perspective that really no one else in that company has. Yet I have never once been asked my point of view about that company from my outside perspective!

Your clients, suppliers, and consultants are your human-centered outside network.

They understand your company but also have an outsider's point of view. Invite them into the problem-finding process. Let them help you see what you cannot see. The days of understanding your business as a manifestation of your own presumed greatness are long gone.

Instead, make sure your thinking throughout this process is customer — not company — centered. Disruption is the time and place to design a new way forward.

WALKING THE WALK

As for me, I knew I had to change from a marketing communications firm into something else. I knew I didn't want to get into the data analytics business. And I knew I did not want to focus 100% on internal communications. So now what?

My business did evolve over time as we did more consulting work, but our earlier clients still saw us as designers who made things in marketing communications. I knew I needed to change but I didn't know how to make that happen or what the change should look like. How might we better serve clients in the Fourth Industrial Revolution? How are clients' needs changing? Outside of marketing communications, what did I need to learn about? What was the market need? Which industries more affected by disruption than others might we work for? Lots of questions, not a lot of answers.

My leadership coach always tells me to focus on the things I have control over and not on the things I don't. But when the world is changing so fast, it's not always possible to determine what those things are.

Orange Square had always helped companies find and solve problems; that's what we do. But doing the thing we do for everyone else in our own firm was another matter. I didn't have an outside perspective. I was too close to the problem. I lacked a clear understanding of the right problem to solve.

I chose not to quit or take a job working for someone else. I chose to set out to change what we do and in the process, stay present to what I was learning.

First, I had to pause and reflect. If I were going to start again, I needed to use what years of experience had taught me. In this process of redefining my business, I also wanted to discover what my leadership position could be. What have I learned from 26 years of working in creative services, founding a company and running it for 17 years? What do I truly believe in and why? In what am I an expert? How do I know this?

That is how this book came about. This is my process of discovery: starting a dialogue with leaders, learning by listening, and giving myself the time to design a new path forward.

As I was negotiating this undertaking, I applied to the Goldman Sachs 10,000 Small Business Program. Babson College had created the curriculum for this program, in which you create a growth opportunity for your company. It was designed like a mini MBA; once you have your idea, you take it through a series of nine modules.

I was accepted in the second cohort in Rhode Island, along with 30 other business owners. We had classroom discussions, peer-learning exercises, skills building and experiential applications. Taught by master teachers, it was one of the best executive learning opportunities I have ever participated in.

TOGETHER WE WENT THROUGH EACH MODULE:

1. You and your business
2. Growth and opportunities
3. Money and metrics
4. You're the leader
5. It's the people
6. Marketing and selling
7. Strategic growth through operations
8. Being bankable
9. Actions for growth

Ideally, by the end of the program, you had a bankable business plan.

Aside from carving out time to work *on* my business rather than just *in* my business, the program offered me what I really needed: other business owners able to offer outside perspectives. Our cohort was divided up into/assigned a growth group — the four people seated at my table. Mine consisted of a nurse, a bike shop owner, an advertising executive, and a real estate developer. So one person was in my industry but had a different background than mine, and the three other people likely knew little about my industry. This was just what I needed.

The growth opportunity we were to propose needed to be predicated on something new. I had to find a new problem to solve. I thought a lot about what Orange Square does and realized that I needed to do something more than tweak things or add a new component. *I had to fundamentally redefine the business.* I had been changing Orange Square over time, and now I had to explain to my growth group what we *really* did, and what made us unique in the marketing communication space.

I was also assigned a business advisor and had to explain the growth opportunity to him as well. When I met with him to discuss what we had been doing, he said it sounded like I was a business consultancy, not a marketing firm.

I had my growth group come to the office, where I showed them a recent project we had completed in which I'd used one of our firm's consulting tools in a new way. I could see they were impressed, but I could see it was also confusing for them: too complex, too much out of the realm of their own business practices. In fact, I was using consulting tools to problem find for a five billion dollar business that was combining services to create something new. But the client was not *really* hiring us to find invisible problems; I was just doing it because I knew this is what we needed to do to produce the results they were after. I was testing and using tools in new ways, and although I couldn't clearly express this new way of working at the time, the results were transformative for the company. But it was not marketing.

In this process of trying to find a growth opportunity predicated on something new, I looked at the different services we provided. Over time we had discovered and developed many tools that we use to help companies uncover hidden problems and discover and define their organizational value. We never did design without a strategy, but selling the strategy was always a challenge because no one wants to buy process. Clients would come to us assuming they already knew the correct problem to solve. Our approach was and is first to discover whether the problem they had identified was, in fact, the correct one to focus on. Our experience over years of strategic problem finding is now part of our standard process and approach. This process is not only one of co-creation, but it is also client-centered and iterative — this is how we get results that distinguish us from other firms.

So I started using our methods on myself to determine what my growth opportunity might be. Given the way product delivery in my business had been transformed by data analytics — and my own disinterest in that practice — I realized that what I had to offer was not design informed by strategic tools, but strategic tools supported by design.

Changing my perspective changed everything. Having to describe what we do to people outside my industry had given me a new perspective as well.

I inverted my business from a brand identity design and marketing services company to a consultancy focused on guiding brands undergoing significant change. We would use our expertise in visualization to create shared meaning within the company and a new understanding of the nature of the challenges they face. BINGO!!!

I researched consulting firms and found that the global management and consulting firm McKinsey & Company's fastest-growing division was design think-ing. And they weren't the only business consultancy getting into design. It was great to see that design had finally arrived on the business scene, confirming what all designers know: that design and design thinking create real, tangible value.

Design is much more than just a pretty-making activity; it's a business innovation powerhouse.

I started reading the articles and whitepapers major consultancies were publishing. They advocated putting the customer first. (*Hmm*, I thought, *there's an idea*! LOL) It was entertaining to read their articles and see how they presented such concepts to the business community. We can now all work in *sprints* to get things done, and we're no longer selling to a customer with whom we don't have to engage, we need to bring *empathy* into the organization, we need *top-line growth, bottom-line efficiency.*

This was the first time I had read these concepts presented from the perspective of a business consulting firm, not a design firm. I had been trained as a designer and been living 100% in a design-driven culture using design thinking for almost 30 years. And yet seeing these concepts co-opted by business consultancies was validating. For years I had wanted to be able to express to clients the inherent values of design as more than pretty-making. If it takes the likes of McKinsey & Company to spread the concept of design thinking in the business world, so be it.

And yet some 25 years ago, David Kelly of IDEO (my hero) was already promoting design in the business world. His company brought the term "Design Thinking" to life by codifying a method and formalizing it into an innovative business process for product development. One of the things I love about design-thinking is that it's project-based learning, something you can apply to everything. Design thinking approaches creative problem-solving in a human-centered way. Kelly promotes the idea that everyone is creative — and they are, which is why it's vital to engage everyone in the process of identifying problems and solving them.

For years, I have been applying design thinking principles to solve the challenges that business-to-business companies face. Organizational-level complexity is, of course, different from product development, where you've already identified the problem you want to solve.

In business service organizations, identifying the right problem is, as I've said, the first challenge.

Through all of this work, what became clear is that I am an expert in problem finding at the organizational and project levels. This is an entirely different proposition from product development, where the product you are making is addressing a defined goal or need. And yet so often in the past, clients approached me intent on a product that I would produce for them. They clearly assumed this product — a website, a brochure, a marketing campaign — to be the solution to their problem.

In earlier years, I simply went ahead and met their stated needs, even if I felt they were solving the wrong problem. But what happens when you deliver the product as requested and the expected results don't follow? That first rule I learned in design school, "You can't find a solution until you have a clearly defined problem," as ever rang true. And yet as self-evident as that may seem, when I tried to engage clients in a discussion about their presumed goal, they looked askance at me, as though I had strayed out of my lane. In many instances the response I got was some version of *Kristine, look around, we have a lot of really smart people in our company. Do you really think we don't know what we want and need?*

Innovation in Business Today

Life in the Fourth Industrial Revolution is more complicated than before. It's not just that the terms of conducting business have changed; the complexity of problems have grown, too, as has what's at stake in their solution. Yes, you can fail and fail fast — but how much better to do that conceptually, *before* you invest significant resources in a mistaken assumption. The fact is, change today happens infinitely faster and with infinitely greater consequences than ever before.

For a business to sustain growth, innovation is required now more than ever. Yet many industries are steeped in tradition and led by baby boomers and Gen Xers. Innovation may be desired — but the risk and process that come with it are not. It's not hard to understand this resistance. Successful business leaders who are now at the sunset of their careers have done things in ways that have worked for years, but the top-down ethos that characterizes that generation is no longer sustainable. There have been tremendous changes in our culture *and* in business, and the two are connected. Integral to success today are conversation and transparency — and that conversation must entail genuine listening, and that transparency must cut across all levels.

Design thinking might be all the rage these days, but are conventional business leaders actually prepared to embrace the human-centered ethos people who are trained in design espouse?

Are you prepared to fail trying, over and over?

Are you willing to embrace the notion that you can't find a solution until you have a clearly defined problem from the customer's point of view?

Are you willing to invest the time these efforts take?

Further complicating the matter is that "delighting the customer" is ever-changing and ever harder as expectations rise and rise. Amazon Prime has gone from delighting people with two-day delivery to delighting them with Amazon Prime one-hour delivery.

One trend as of late is that businesses are buying design firms. One of the challenges I see is that they want to use design thinking to empower innovation, but lack a culture of engaging productively with failure and change. For the longest time, leaders have been taught that projecting strength leads to success, but in truth, what it leads to is rigidity.

To relinquish that posture and operate from a place of vulnerability is what is needed in today's business culture.

You can't command trained designers to solve your problem — not if you really want to solve the real problem — but you *can* engage thoughtfully with the design team, focusing on finding the *right* problem before seeking a solution and permitting the time to solve it. Because that reflex to instantly solve a problem as soon as it appears, too, is also a symptom of the arrogance born of projecting strength.

A Look in the Mirror Before Moving Forward

With respect to my own business, I had to pause and consider whether I, a Gen Xer myself, nonetheless at times carried myself unwittingly in a similar manner. For me to reflect on myself in this way was all the more difficult because I was at a perilous juncture in my professional career and in my business. My growth opportunity, which at first I had only focused on in strictly business terms, was, in fact, an opportunity for *personal* growth. Change would have to come from within me, too.

As for my business, I wanted to work with C-level Gen X leaders who had never conducted their business in conventional terms, leaders who understood that what worked in the past isn't going to work in the future.

I wanted to help them activate a growth opportunity they had chosen as vital to their success. It's an approach that resonates with their millennial work-force who'll get behind a purpose-driven concept and work to make it succeed, as long as they're truly invested in the project and able to bring their best talents to fruition.

Everyone wants to feel valued at work, and everyone wants to add value. Once you have identified a clear goal, then you can co-create and further refine that goal, and thereby achieve greater success. When you work together to develop the principles and standards for how you will do this work and check in along the way to ensure that the principles and standards everyone agreed to are being met, and when people can see the importance of their contributions, lots of positive learning takes place. People can then organize around the work that needs to get done, connecting their identities and values with the project.

I worked on my growth opportunity in the Goldman Sachs 10,000 small business program until I had a bankable idea. I didn't need investments, but I did need new customers. I had no idea what potential clients would think about my new services. Is this something they would buy? How much would they pay? How do these leaders choose their growth opportunities?

I had what I believe was a good idea, but I still had questions that needed answering. I didn't have enough information to make a value proposition design for my idea; that is, determine where what I offer intersects with what clients need. So I used my clients and their connections to solicit feedback about my idea. I started with customers who knew me. They gave me great feedback, saying I had something to offer for which there was a need. I would ask them to refer me to someone else, so I could keep learning. As I started talking to business leaders who did not know who I was or anything about my company, they naturally went to my website. When I met with them, I could feel the disconnect between what they saw there — a marketing communications website — and the growth opportunity I was talking to them about — a consultancy. My intention was to create a new brand separate from Orange Square, but with all that I had learned, I knew I needed to change Orange Square first.

I hired a top consultant in our industry, and he could not help me better position Orange Square. This was disappointing but, in a way, illuminating. As it turned out, Orange Square didn't have a raft of immediately identifiable issues, but instead a conceptual conundrum — and one he seemed unable to solve, which put the problem back on me. Thinking more carefully about my growth opportunity finally yielded clarity on what we actually had been doing for years: We didn't simply design brand identities, we guided companies through significant brand transitions.

I learned/realized that we bring clarity to changing brands. We are experts at organizational-level change following a merger, acquisition or new CEO. Companies that are undergoing this kind of significant change face branding challenges on many levels, so clearly there's a lot at stake.

I REDEFINED OUR SERVICES IN THREE SEQUENTIAL CATEGORIES:

- Discovering Organizational Value
- Defining Organizational Value
- Delivering Organizational Value

This new understanding bridged the gap between my growth opportunity and my company itself. I also realized (mercifully) that I might not have to make another brand. For now, it all fit within the purview of Orange Square. In effect, I experienced firsthand — and successfully overcame — my clients' predicament.

Here Are Some Actionable Steps I Took in My Process. I Hope You Will Find Them Valuable.

1. I worked to state my problem and then to refine and restate it by breaking it into parts, trying to identify possible growth opportunities. (My problem was that the industry had shifted to data analytics and I wasn't interested in doing data analytics. So what would I do instead that would have value for a client and meaning for me? Only after finally defining the discrete aspects of our services did it become clear that consulting about change at an organizational level would be the focus of my growth opportunity.)

2. I identified a new growth opportunity, and that gave me a fresh perspective on my company and thereby, the conceptual means to effect change and growth.

3. I flipped what we were doing as a company on its head. (We had been a branding firm with a focus on marketing communication hired principally to market brands, during the process of which we used consulting tools to understand the changes that our clients faced.

   Now we're a consultancy principally focused on helping brands at significant points of change negotiate that change through visualization, design thinking methods, and organizational clarity tools. In effect, we're no longer focused on a product but on the process, ensuring companies identify the right problems before investing in solving the wrong ones.)

4. I changed my perspective by going outside my sector and doing research on business consulting firms, as well as by looking at how traditional consulting firms like McKensey had launched design thinking services.

5. For months I dwelled in the discomfort of the unknown — and gave myself space and time for the ideas I needed to take shape without being

forced. (Ideas come to you in between the things you are doing.)

6. I allowed myself and everyone on the team to be vulnerable. I went "all in" even if it meant I might fail trying.

7. I made my ideas visible. I sketched them out and had my designers draw the concepts I was trying to convey. My entire growth opportunity was rendered in visuals.

8. I conducted interviews with leaders going through change, allowing me to define and restate the problems from a different perspective — that is, from a potential customer's point of view.

9. I did a lot of thinking about something by not thinking about it and did things I enjoy that had nothing to do with work.

10. I explored many ideas that didn't work, so I was failing and learning all of the time.

11. I stayed curious and got feedback from people

outside my industry, including my Goldman Sachs growth group, advisors, and friends.

12. I condensed my 26 years of experience into a 15-minute talk at a design week conference and solicited feedback, which helped me gain greater clarity on how I'm perceived professionally, and also helped me position myself as something more than a designer.

13. I had — and still have — an entire idea wall where I write ideas on index cards and sticky notes along with visuals. I am always looking for patterns. The first one I saw was Failure, Problems, and Change, which is how I recognized the true nature of my professional calling.

14. I invited other people to look at the wall and tell me what they saw.

15. When I thought I had the answers, I found some one with a totally different perspective and invited them into the process.

16. In my ongoing interviews, I continue to learn about the value of what I seek to offer from the customer's point of view, and then I refine the offer accordingly.

The Difference Between Corporate-Centered and Human-Centered Thinking

CORPORATE-CENTERED THINKING

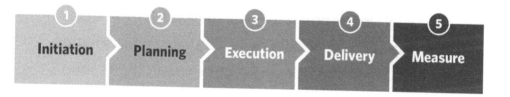

In corporate-centered thinking, a company starts with a goal and moves through the process of attempting to achieve that goal in a linear fashion, one stage building on the next. This process usually mirrors the corporate structure, starting at the top and moving down through the organizational structure. It begins with an assessment of business requirements and an initiation of ideas to meet those requirements, that is, a perceived solution to the perceived problem. Next,

it moves on to planning the project, including time-
frame and budget. Then executing the solution(s),
followed by delivery marketing and selling to achieve
the intended goal. It is at this point you measure how
your solution is received. It is also at this point you
learn whether you have deficits in results, meaning
the offer is not being received in the way you expected.
Then you set out to refine the solutions based on
critical feedback from your intended audience.

All of the time and money that went into the five
stages of development of course cast a long shadow
over the process of refining or changing your solution.
Indeed, the more time and money spent, the harder
it is to make changes. How far back in the process are
you willing to go to fix or refine the solution? Which
part is to blame for the deficit in results? The steps
at the end are easier to focus on than the first step,
the goal itself, in part because the farther back you go
in the process the higher up you go in the company.
People at the bottom don't have the same power, so
asking a question like: "Where did the goal come from
in the first place?" makes no sense. But it's hard to go
back to the initiation step where people at the top of
the company developed the idea, because now you're

blaming the boss and that's usually off-limits. So the easiest steps to address are those at the end of the process. Start with marketing and selling, and see if you can get better results. At least you stand to gain more information about what is working and what is not, since they are on the front lines with customers. If after you have worked on marketing and selling, you still have a deficit, it is at this point you have to accept that the solution itself needs to be addressed. But as I said, moving back this far is not something that most people are willing to stomach. So, it's not hard to see that corporate-centered thinking is fundamentally flawed.

Corporate-Centered

 Start with a Goal

Initiation
Ideas for achieving goals

Planning
Choosing Solution(s)

Execution
Making the Solution(s)

Delivery
Marketing / Selling Solution(s)

Measure

 End with Audience

HUMAN-CENTERED THINKING

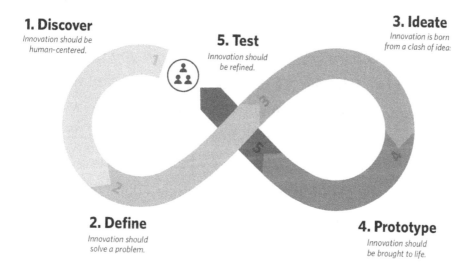

1. Discover
Innovation should be human-centered.

5. Test
Innovation should be refined.

3. Ideate
Innovation is born from a clash of idea:

2. Define
Innovation should solve a problem.

4. Prototype
Innovation should be brought to life.

Human-centered thinking, on the other hand, uses a design thinking framework for innovation that starts and ends with the audience, and is an infinite feedback loop of learning and improvement, not a linear process predicated on assumptions. It starts with the problem(s) your clients have. In the discovery phase, you are using empathy, understanding, and discovery to focus on problem finding, expanding what you know by gathering more information and learning from your clients. In the discovery process, you gain insights that allow you to identify the problem(s) you need to solve from the many choices you have. Once you have defined the problem(s), you ideate. What are the different approaches you can take to solve your problem(s)? What is needed, what is possible? Then you design a solution and prototype that solution — this is where you are focusing on how you can best solve your client's issue or pain points. You work with your clients to see whether what you have designed or developed is in fact what they need. You test and refine, always going you back to where you started: the client. It is a process of expansion and refinement in each phase.

Human-Centered

Start with the Problems Your Audience Has

Discover
Empathy, Understanding, Discovery, Insight, Defining Problems

Problem Finding

Problem Definition

Design
Different approaches that can be taken.
Designing Solution(s)

Ideate

Connecting Problems and Solutions

Prototype

Deliver
Testing

Test

End with Audience

In the fourth industrial revolution, business has become too complex and everything is moving and changing at too fast a pace to assume at the outset that you know which problem(s) to solve. That of course is precisely the folly of a corporate-centered approach. A human-centered approach on the other hand makes no such assumptions and instead solicits ideas from the people being served.

When it comes to thought leadership, marketing and selling, the human-centered approach offers a huge bonus. Because this process is based on a deep understanding of your client's needs, you know what to write about for your thought leadership. Because what you have created is what clients need, you are not going to discover at the end of your process that what you have created has insufficient service or offer. You have also solved the problem of dealing with the power dynamics of a corporate structure that you cannot control or overcome by putting the client at the center and not the company itself. Everyone imagines they want to be client-centered or patient-centered or human-centered but if you set goals from a corporate-centered perspective you will never truly achieve that goal.

"Failure is a good preparation for success, which comes as a pleasant surprise, but success is poor preparation for failure."

—Sarah Manguso, *300 Arguments*

Diversity, Inclusion, and Openness

The shift from corporate-centered thinking to human-centered thinking is reflective of a change in genera-tional thinking. It is about recognizing and embracing the growing diversity in the US. The Baby Boomer generation is 18% non-white.[8] Today Gen Z is 48% non-white.[8] To say that corporate-centered thinking evolved from a patriarchal white point of view is hardly provocative. That was simply the reality of the business world at that time. And now today, even though change happens fast and we need to move at the pace of change, if we continue to use the out-moded, dominance-driven approach of "leadership knows best" to try to foist a new business idea, system, or growth strategy on employees, we will continue to solve the wrong problem and get the wrong answer, and waste time and money in the process. When we look at the diversity numbers in the US alone, we see how our employees and customers have changed. We need to match that change, using

US GENERATIONS BY SIZE AND DIVERSITY

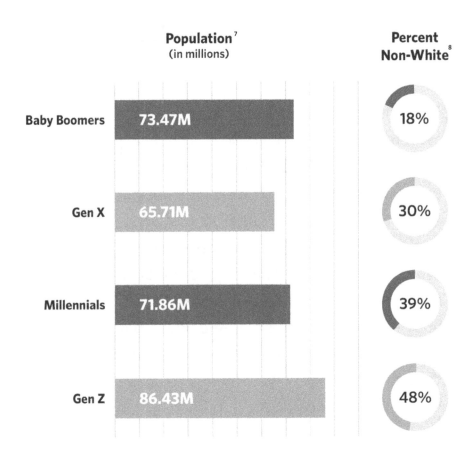

Population[7]
(in millions)

Percent
Non-White[8]

Baby Boomers	73.47M	18%
Gen X	65.71M	30%
Millennials	71.86M	39%
Gen Z	86.43M	48%

7 Fry, Richard. "Millennials projected to overtake Baby Boomers as America's largest generation" Pew Research Center, 1 Mar. 2018, https://www.pewresearch.org/fact-tank/2018/03/01/millennials-over-take-baby-boomers.

8 Fry, Richard. Parker, Kim. "Early Benchmarks Show 'Post-Millennials' on Track to Be Most Diverse, Best-Educated Generation Yet" Pew Research Center, 15 Mar. 2018, https://www.pewsocialtrends.org/2018/11/15/early-benchmarks-show-post-millennials-on-track-to-be-most-diverse-best-educated-generation-yet.

human-centered thinking to drive value, inclusion, equity, and connection. Taking the time to truly listen to others allows us to learn when our initial assumptions are in fact limited or mistaken. It allows us to consider things we didn't even know, and it allows us to learn and grow — and apologize when our words or actions offend others.

Customers know what they need and want — you just have to find out what that is. With human-centered thinking using diverse teams of employees and customers, you uncover hidden problems at a faster pace. Your teams can then focus on assessing your current services, finding gaps and creating new services.

Of course, you must first begin by understanding the value proposition of each service, that is the connection between your service — the pain relievers and benefits it offers — and your customer's job — the pains they are experiencing and the outcomes they need to achieve — and then recognizing where the two intersect. The only way to do this is through human-centered thinking. The marketing team and designers can then use their talents and systems to attract your tribe and achieve shared goals.

In the Fourth Industrial Revolution, customers, employees and leadership will have no choice but to innovate and design a new way forward, working together to build an authentic brand from the outside in. From there it becomes easier to attract employees dedicated to the mission, and their work then becomes all the more meaningful for them.

I believe that leaders who build internal teams by focusing on diversity and inclusion will have a competitive advantage in problem finding. Leaders who create cultures of problem finding by focusing on clients will save money and time and have more success.

And still, successful businesses do require leadership, and it's hard to be the kind of leader who has the guts, grit and determination to slow things down. Remember ideas come in between the things you do.

- Take walks and let your mind wander
- Exercise
- Put your phone away
- Seek wisdom, stillness and quiet
- Be present
- Revisit your values

- Zoom out
- Learn to say no
- Get some sleep
- Detach from outcomes
- Ask important questions:
  - Do I/we need to do this?
  - Will this matter in 5 years?
  - What if I do nothing?
  - What am I working on in myself today?
  - Why do I care what others think?
  - What is the worst thing that can happen?
  - What is the best thing that can happen?

Be steady and act with clarity amid the frenzy. Hear what needs to be heard. Step back and reflect. Practice gratitude and kindness. Model vulnerability, so that everyone can join in with you on the journey. **Make a difference in the most human-centered way possible.**

About the Author

Kristine Merz is the Founder and President of Orange Square. For the past 27 years, Kristine's focus has been on audience-centered marketing communication, brand strategy, brand identity, and business success. As a battle-tested entrepreneur, Kristine's focus has been on B2B companies that are experiencing significant points of change. She uses design thinking and human-centered design methods to bring clarity to change while helping companies move through a brand transformation and design a new way forward.

A classically trained designer from the Rhode Island School of Design, Kristine has been recognized seven times for outstanding brand repositioning by REBRAND 100® Global Awards, the highest juried recognition for brand transformations in the world. She is a Graduate of the Goldman Sachs 10,000 Small Business program.

SHIFT

About Orange Square

Orange Square is a human-centered brand and business strategy firm that helps businesses navigate through significant points of change. Whether experiencing a merger or acquisition, leadership change, disruption in the market, or rapid growth, you need a customer-centered approach to solve the right problems. At Orange Square, our approach to tackling periods of change is founded on the principles of human-centered design and design thinking. Our business consulting tools can help to uncover and define the business challenges clients are facing in order to express the most accurate and engaging visual identity.

Engaging a uniquely-applied design thinking methodology ensures success by identifying the right problem, not solving the wrong one. We help bring clarity to organizational change by Discovering, Defining, and Delivering Organizational Value. Our tested methods help clients to better define and integrate organizational value on three levels: leadership, employees, and clients.

Using this uniquely individualized lens, we build business value and accelerate growth by creating and managing integrated brand experiences across all touchpoints. Bridging business strategy and design, we create solutions that engage people in the most effective way possible.

Orange Square is a certified WBENC woman-owned business.

NOTES:

NOTES:

NOTES:

CPSIA information can be obtained
at www.ICGtesting.com
Printed in the USA
LVHW031838160320
650186LV00012B/1276